# PRESS RELEASE

| | |
|---|---|
| Title: | *Particulars of Place* |
| Author: | Richard O. Moore |
| Edited by: | Garrett Caples<br>Paul Ebenkamp<br>Brenda Hillman |
| Pub Date: | April 2015 |
| ISBN: | 978-1-63243-005-2 |
| Genre: | Poetry |
| Price: | $17.95, trade paperback, 6" x 9" |
| Page Count: | 96 |
| Publisher: | Omnidawn Publishing |
| Distributor: | University Press of New England Book Partners |
| Previous Books by Author: | *Writing the Silences* (University of California Press, 2010) |
| Honors Include: | Co-founder of KPFA, a listener-sponsored radio station |
| Director of: these films: | *Take this Hammer* (featuring James Baldwin, 1963)<br>*Louisiana Diary* (documenting CORE voter registration drive, 1963)<br>*USA: Poetry* (which contains the only sound footage of Frank O'Hara, 1966)<br>*Love You Madly* (with Duke Ellington, 1967)<br>*A Concert of Sacred Music* (with Duke Ellington, 1967)<br>*The Writer in America* (1975) |
| Contact Person: | Rusty Morrison, Omnidawn Publishing |
| For Further Info: | rusty@omnidawn.com,<br>(800) 792-4957, ext. 4<br>Fax: (510) 232-8525 |

# Particulars
## of
## Place

## by Richard O. Moore

Edited by:
Garrett Caples
Paul Ebenkamp
Brenda Hillman

Book cover art and design by Janet Tumpich


Cover typeface: Adobe Jenson Pro.
Interior Typefaces: Trajan Pro and Adobe Garamond Pro


Each Omnidawn author participates fully in the design of his or her book,
choosing cover art and design and approving cover and interior design.
Omnidawn strives to create books that align with each author's vision.


Offset printed in the United States
by Edwards Brothers Malloy, Ann Arbor, Michigan
On 55# Enviro Natural 100% Recycled 100% PCW
Acid Free Archival Quality FSC Certified Paper
with Rainbow FSC Certified Colored End Papers


Library of Congress Cataloging-in-Publication Data


Published by Omnidawn Publishing, Richmond, California
www.omnidawn.com    (510) 237-5472    (800) 792-4957
10  9  8  7  6  5  4  3  2  1
ISBN: 978-1-63243-005-2

For Flinn, David, Lisa, Michael, Anthony, Aran

# CONTENTS

IV.

V.

# INTRODUCTION
## BY CEDAR SIGO

"And the insects of a day die in the starlight," Rexroth's dead-on summary;
we have followed all signs into the cities of others,
occupied the palaces, the public squares,
our natural policy is forced entry and what comes after,
we have stared into the eyes of hatred and wondered why we are not loved.
In the catalogue of atrocities no one is spared.
There are no good wishes in a time of war and the first fatality is prayer.
Richard O. Moore, "Particulars of Place"

Richard O. Moore's achievements will always breathe an air of the unreal. I first knew his work as a filmmaker, primarily his portraits of poets from the mid 1960s for KQED. The series was titled *Poetry: USA*, ten films including Robert Duncan, John Wieners, and the only sound synched film of Frank O'Hara. These portraits provide completely natural, indelible footage of the poets in their element. Wieners reads to us from a fire and smoke damaged room at the Hotel Wentley. I remember most clearly his reading of *The Address of the Watchman to the Night* being intercut with a long shot of Polk street, the camera speeding by from the passenger side capturing silhouettes of strangers walking or trapped in windows, blurred store fronts and bright neon letters against black. These were happenstance scenes still particular to Wieners narration,

> To explore those dark eternals of the night-world: the prostitute, the dope
> addict, thief and pervert. These were the imagined heroes of my world:
> and the orders of my life. What they stood for, how they lived, what they
> did in the daytime were the fancies of my imagination. And I had to
> become everyone of them until I knew.

My favorite scene in the O'Hara film is his rapid fire dialogue laid onto paper as it's brought to mind with the painter Alfred Leslie, the phone rings, Frank answers and it's hard to say if they seem more or less aware of the camera. We are let so completely into their lives. We learn that our daydreams of legendary poets hardly begin to do them justice. His film of Ed Sanders includes footage (inside and out) of The Peace Eye Bookstore. Did I imagine the smoke billowing out the front window? What I find most commendable about the *USA: Poetry* series is Richard's choice to showcase so many heroes of the queer underworld and without a trace of tokenism. His mindset dates extremely well. One would be hard pressed to find another man so unencumbered by social divisions. Richard is humble in person but his work and what it attempts are fierce almost dangerous dreams. The dimensions of his life form a perfect flickering screen for poetry.

At first light
Fact follows fact
Into the visible

Point to it
Before the words
Begin the pretense
That language
Is a picture
Of the world
And God is all
That is the case

Inside the language game
There is no room for doubt,

Change the rules or stay
Indentured to God forever

Enrolling at Berkeley in the late 1930s, Moore first studied poetry under Josephine Miles and eventually found himself among the anarchist-libertarian circle of Kenneth Rexroth. This group would at various times include editor George Leite, Tom Parkinson and Philip Lamantia. Though he did publish his poetry in the early Bay area magazines *Circle* and *Ark*, it would seem that publishing was never too high a priority for Richard. *Particulars of Place* is only his second book. *Writing the Silences* was published by University of California Press in 2010, edited by Brenda Hillman and Paul Ebenkamp from over sixty years of writing. The book includes a chronological introduction finally recognizing Richard as a true poet of the San Francisco Renaissance. We should consider ourselves fortunate to be writing during the publication of Richard's second volume. He is possessed of one of the most spontaneous, joyful lines I have ever encountered. I first got to know him making visits to his home in Mill Valley with the poet Garrett Caples. We would talk about whatever we were each working on but soon the afternoon would evolve into reading each other's new work aloud. While some poets are silenced by the hush around a reader ending a poem, this moment always seems to excite Richard. He can find immediate handles or questions for lines that are still hanging in the air. It gets to the point that I begin to feel prideful, reminded that we are together reading and speaking what is essentially a hidden, highly wrought language. It demands intimacy at even the most oblique passages. Richard seems to go someplace else when reading his poetry. It becomes clear when hearing him how much the reading aloud of the poem must inform the editing, the audible turns and inlaid surprise of the humor depend on the voice finding its most flattering, heated distance from the content.

> It is a misdirected enterprise to call upon the dead for wisdom
> we have their words but the speakers are just that: dead
> along with their enfeebled gods and ghostly shrines
> yet the sword slices the same meat of the same animal
> that fought at Troy and the ghost that rushes from us is the same.
>
> We have our seasons and our instruments of perishable joy
> our shadow metaphysic of the transient soul
> our virtual realities dislodge the arbitrary gods.
> We build our temples with the stones at hand.

Charles Olson, William Carlos Williams and Ludwig Wittgenstein are divided equally in Richard's voice. He has never feared dealing with the content of epic. Dizzying views of history and mythology are uncovered, enshrined and as quickly shut down, crushed in rhyme and resurrected through wit. The symbols slowly come to greet us in the title poem, *Particulars of Place,* as it becomes an interactive map of sorts. He knows exactly what figures, shades or animals should populate his works and his diction shelters them all with a round containment. This book is divided into six sections. Their length and relative variety give the feel of intense fits of writing issued as separate short books. It's as if Richard has continually reintroduced himself to his practice through the apprehension of new forms. The numbered prose poems entitled DELETE find him utilizing a computerized voice, darting the corners of the bright screen with relentless black humor. The last sequence, *Outcry: Blindness Sonnets,* melds the loss of eyesight to the absolute need to memorize and press poetry straight into his speaking voice, it's the realization that what wants to be said must be remembered. The course of these sonnets can truly be traced to Olson's "the heart by way of breath to the line."

VI

"Get used to it." No, I won't.
This was all I could think of while
Passing through a well remembered door
(it opens in not out, there is no sill)
A detail now wrapped in layers of gauze
Plus endless other unrealities.
This has become the order of the day
And every day now on against my will

To have it otherwise would now be called
An optical illusion. You can pass through
A solid wall, all it takes is a single door.
A negotiation with reality
Is to ride the in-breath into death, blind
I long for that other-sighted world still.

Richard O. Moore is exemplary in his openness. His poetry is rooted in places with bass notes that are impossible to skim, they magnetize our voice and the whole of his life comes to bear in whatever the measure has conjured. The strength of his commitment assures that no false note can ever be sounded. It's as if the poetry were protected by a vision, a brand of verse that may actually come true following its assembly and publication. This collection seems the perfect answer to Philip Lamantia's open question, "Isn't poetry the dream of weapons?"

1

# PARTICULARS OF PLACE

*"There were two ravens sat on a tree ...*
The one of them said to his mate
where shall we our breakfast take?
with a down, derry, derry
down, down."*

## ONE

Delusional histories
        in closed minds or broken
        claim us
        as their own.

Pound in his Pisan cage
memories
        in the heat
        like flies

a mad old man
        in parallel worlds
        no history
nor fortune     nor clear name to come.

*Death, sweet lover, gently give me ease.*

\*\*\*

Shake the rattle of entrances: "Stately...Buck Mulligan"
descends and languages gather to speak of a world
with nowhere to go except into the open
into the artifice of a known predictable world.

History, a carrion discourse of accident
and ignorance, base pairs ascending—descending
ladders of life, the story recited in names of places
where they died. Agamemnon, in a bathtub.

History as disambiguation
replication virus of memory
that eats, *phage,* yes
eats what there is to know.
The carrion crow and skylark a constellation
imposed against the certainty of stars.

✳✳✳

In footnotes only a library of cruelty
in whispers barely speakable acts
that disabuse the householder from the human house
the human from a shared and animal home.

Propose a measurable landscape
a cell in its own life-cycle dying
these certainties tumbled and bound
make up the case this daily show that is the world.

In whatever language spoken.

✳✳✳

Move the levers
that guide the bird
fix the target
release the Word.
the Word destroys
with techno-skill
the target plus
collateral.

✳✳✳

Speak of an agony and anesthesia
follows like a perfect dog at heel
returning same place same day next year.
mandalas of history never learned.

King Priam humbled before the MVP
of that war brought back the husk of a son
and was on Troy's last day at random gutted
by Achilles' son learning the craft of war.

Same story in a different language told.
Hector dragged through Fallujah once again.

*** *** ***

Old Coyote  you trick me with your dreams
in the desert  my insomnia hears you howling

and all of which seems  this morning to be me
goes traveling with the Old Man  "we must find water"
this is what he says in the arroyos

                    O my prince of paradox
your hide is mangy and you smell.

# Two

Bring to the common table all we have
the sum outright of possibility
fleshed in the words that move among us

    A claptrap way of speaking
    vague as political speech
    sentimental at the quick of it
    with violence as the engine of the heart
    the future is not a thought experiment

I cannot name a warring state my own
nor swear allegiance to a nation's flag.

*** 

Under incoming fire, the warrior's perfected community of trust
and mutual aid, trust is both ends and means in a survival game,
history's long traverse across the killing fields, army against army
on the desolate plains, or in another country selecting death by remote control
is to end in the kingdom of the absurd which is exactly where we are.
How step outside locksteps of time, the long march into desolation
which is history, a step not out of nature but into the possibility
of steps that do not follow what has come before.

"And the insects of a day die in the starlight," Rexroth's dead-on summary;
we have followed all signs into the cities of others,
occupied the palaces, the public squares,
our natural policy is forced entry and what comes after,
we have stared into the eyes of hatred and wondered why we are not loved.
In the catalogue of atrocities no one is spared.
There are no good wishes in a time of war and the first fatality is prayer.

Lord Krishna spoke of the world as it is, the cycles of death and the terrible
command to be as you are, spoken to Arjuna warrior without choice.
Another absolute at work in the absolute limits
of an absolute life. *As you are*, a command to press toward death
until death and birth are let go in a Disneyworld of fulfilled fantasies

the ultimate suspension of belief and none of the crossroad signs predict
where we may go. There is always an alternate text.
Let the gods fight their battles to the death of gods.

✺✺✺

To frame the gates
Of paradise
Eternal hopes
From human lies.

Tears of envy
Tears of grief
Feed the flower
Burn the leaf.

Strike the anvil
Shape the wheel
Hammer out
The commonweal.

✺✺✺

*Creatio ex nihilo,* revisited.
Alchemical pretension once again,
A mythic mingling of the heart and head
With prophetic obligations to explain
A pearl of wisdom beyond common price.

> *Pleroma, the fullness*
> *of light and time*
> *and possibility*
> *the voice of Valentinius*

A mouthful surely but never quite enough
To save the sorcerer's apprentice
From the Sorcerer's rebuff.

19

*Only the select achieve it*
*initiate in secret doctrine*
*the Gospel of Thomas*
*the message of Judas Iscariot*

Within the myth of light into eternal light
redemption can be neither lost or won
      so long as ash from Troy obscures the morning sun
in restless chaos impenetrable night

*Respect the old books*
*the myths that feed*
*the need to believe*
*and to be comforted*
*with final answers*
*absolute solutions*
*oh beware!*

✳✳✳

From the farthest outpost of the spoken world
stone drawn across stone
glyphs that move among us into words
beginning of culture, calculation, intentional war,
battlefields of relatives; dharma, dharma,
we are related in our common blood, there is no death
we cannot call our own.

*And "that which is the case"*
*remains as rage sets fire*
*to fire. and speech becomes*
*all shopworn sentiment.*

Beyond Kandahar on orders of the State
young men walk with fire beneath each step
their life held breathless in a void of sense
but deep in understanding of the dark.

# THREE

Familiars of vision: heron in a quicksilver pool,
snow in a silver bowl, pulse and the departure of time.

At Green Gulch, two owls on a cypress limb
one facing east, the other west. Sitting
consumed in quiet apart from the wind,
a misplacement, coincidence without intent
until now. Yes. There they are:
two owls in a veil of fog. Leave it. Move on
into the uproar that is the world,
a chatter of leaf against leaf, an audible mist
in the trees, there is no moment of rest
in a restless, disinterested world.

And therein are the wars, the stretches of peace,
strategic advantage, counterinsurgency, massacre,
genocide, ceasefire, the abstract language
of the State nourished in blood and policy
in stretches of peace and in moments of red mist.
Without seeming to move, an owl calls from a cypress tree,
come nightfall the owl is a silent killer.

❋❋❋

Balance in the mind
with balance in the heart
read riot in the wind
search order within art.

Water in the spring
poison in the well
a dove upon the wing
a decoy into hell.

The two sides of a coin
one war and one of peace
opposites that join

upon the thumb's release.
One succeeds, one fails
whenever the coin is spun
the world reads heads or tails
the coin remains as one.

\*\*\*

Have you seen the dragon that awakes the world?

Two heads     one facing east     the other west
joined at the communal body     the economy     the state

darkness at first bell     until the dragon rouses
and awakes the east with fire

nonsense in any common way of making sense

answer the bell.

\*\*\*

Language withers upon encounter with a god
hugely present but not here. What follows is never
a matter of waiting for the next event, trashed
bits and pieces of a broken-into world,
accept as you choose from the safety of a point of view,
life is not an hypothesis to be proved.

Our practice: this in-breath of the commonplace,
divine turbulence and terrible freedom of the here and now,
a virtual world of prophetic folly and earthly wisdom
wrapped tight in the lies we tell ourselves
while ignorant of the lies we tell.

2

# DELETE 7

So *mon lecteur* if you insist upon truth at least admit that it must be made up not lying there in wait like a golf ball or an explorer with vision just before death in turn made up by a biographer whose mind was made up before the first sight of snow freedom is all you've got poor thing watch how the local *supermercado* appears infinite to the explorers to those with little or nothing at all : your famine is on TV and what if your *truths* insists upon equality where are you then in the made-up language tour? Cruelty and self-destroying pain need not be delivered by your hand to work their best there are always others for that job "they do it to themselves" is what you'll say yesterdays truths are physics out of date and unemployable but for the moment relax and look outside : storms "batter" the north coast spousal abuse Poseidon Slugs Mother Earth not exactly : Poseidon no longer sells although Odysseus under many an alias is alive as any of the written- up immortals on the page meanwhile attend to the morning shopping list check out TV for rape earthquake and war oh! And don't forget sports with its mortgage points they cost money and why not you'll pay : the ball is in your court dearie decide on a leveraged forehand or an overhead smash too late! the ball that you let go just caught the line its game at love the umpire says and little mirror-face if this won't choke your chicken you'll need a taleteller like Shaun or the other one Shem for after all you are the living breathing tongue-tied son thereof what? Ho? Those bats have come again to show just *you* the entry/exit of what may become your only shelter a survival kit is what you'll need but it won't last long comprised as it is of old assumptions dead you'll need new words for night and strangers armed with all that you don't have switch-a-rooney : tonight's game is the Barbarians versus the Hunkers as a fan watch for rats beneath the seats it adds a certain edge as the pawns are moved : robed Sisters of Mercy care for this crowd long past their hour of bedtime leave theology for what gets trashed avoid contamination the plague changes in fashion tb aids : your flaming cross shows off fresh metal teeth.

# DELETE 8

Have you said your sermon this morning? the road it travels is dusty
and wide and goes round and round and round the mountain to say it
is obvious is to say it is crowded with refugees you and the others on
the road no destination in sight you are alive though boring at times
and the smell of you is instant nausea you breathe white breath in the
early morning air indeed you may have a flair for going round and
round with a skip and a jump at the most unexpected moments wasn't
that you on a music box dancing in perfect porcelain? A quake threw
you from your shelf but round the mountain you must go suppose for
once you went *up* the mountain? would that be a different direction
or just more tiring? would it disturb the order of the ten thousand of
ten thousand things? do you care? do you know whose sermon this is?
it's a habit you'll have for life although things do slow down fall into
themselves and leave the world to silence and to aha? gotcha? you're *it*
for now but it won't be long before another sucker comes this way and
you can hide under the desk with the rest of us : look : sky and sea are
an undifferentiated gray even the birds disappear but forecast faith in a
word and the osprey is there again hanging head-down in the wind it's
plain that being unsure gives you your daily terror you even lift a prayer
for it bells ring and you know it is the buoy off Saunders's Reef the red
light assures you the buoy is still there that no Debussy bells have come
to dismantle your ears you're safe in being where you are not that you've
got a warranty for life no matter what the salesman said you signed up
for Metaphysics I cost a bundle left you high and dry : how dare you
take all hope away? well in the first place it crash landed years ago you've
been standing there imagining greaves breastplate helmet with plumes
the whole she-bang but don't weep today for what you did then there's
a lot to learn about letting go and you won't hear a clang of armor when
you do in your most invincible day you were a larvae underfoot you
lived by chance shape-shifting you are a fortunate one without a shell
no plane overhead gun to your head you are accidentally free in the full
terror of being who you are but tell me now this once and forever have
you built your language out of the things you love?

# DELETE 9

You keeper of coins and keys press on with that cart one wheel not tracking hard to steer pick up some beer some bread some low-fat cheese and split this market for the great and green outdoors : a fast track stimulus/response has brought this jay that you see to this specific tree troubles you doesn't it that you matter not one feather to that bird : mon voyeur : my Wordsworth : please don't mutter teleology like a heathen spell it ill becomes you to speak in tongues all tied together in one noisy lot like jays but hey! comparisons don't wash today so don't be frightened if the walls seem greener than they were before a rainy Tuesday you may recall but that word's not important what's in a name? not much but maybe more than you'll admit like your passport picture that can't possibly be you with that silly smile : nameless you do a modern kind of harm move-on old tool-user to the next aisle it's clear that a balanced checkbook exchange will not turn this trick flatten the hills straighten the curves be intimate as earth and air : nonsense once again : it is hard to make way against history's unfocused projection for instance who have you invited for dinner tonight? A month ago you wrote a name down on your shopping list so much happens between then and now you live with what doesn't care a fig for you floods and earthquakes for starters and there's always the fire you learned in childhood metaphysical flames it's not that you're separate from nature it's just that nature is all you have to live with now : at birth you saw it as the enemy now it's you and all those other mammals so much like you most of them worse off in your popular mechanics commercial for the earth new birth is not an odds-on favorite here you cohabit with the jay a continuum of accident and necessity now the jays have flown to another tree the noises you make little drummer are all noises that have been heard before time for a new tune that can't be played on the old drums but don't expect folks to give up their loyalties their comfort level when they hear your latest noise it is of course the same old tune only distorted re-served : tell me tom or tad or two-penny-tush does anyone understand you enough to say you're selling a scam a fraud although you call it the secret of life?

# DELETE 12

Welcome to your day of sanity! Come in and close the door it will likely lock behind you and you will be home alone waste disposal will take care of your needs : at long last undisturbed phenomena without the heavy metal background of the street will be yours for observation and response : do you have visions? do you think? Your mouth do you open it for more than medication? I should know I know that I should know : we've watched centuries erode the fortress drain the moat the poet's clumsy beast has reached its home and prey we wither in the gridlock of our power only the guns remain and are in use pure accident is beauty to be glimpsed your trembling only further clouds your sight I in my home you in your other place harmonize the fading anthem of an age the cracked bell of our liberty keeps time a penny for the corpse you left behind keep on recycling all that you have heard before call it a double bind much like the deadbolt that locked the door that keeps you safe and sane : ho—hum—harry who? oh that's just a phrase found in a time capsule capped and sealed and shot up in the air : no I cannot tell you where it fell to earth that page was torn out years ago it's chance that we have a fragment of that language left : do your archeology before a mirror the canyons and the barren plains are clear but where to dig for a ruined golden age a fiction we were served with breakfast flakes say have you forgot this day of sanity? No problem the heavy key was thrown away as soon as the door was closed and locked you're safe : some day the asylum may be torn down to make way for a palace of the mad it does not follow that anything will change : choose your executioner by lot almost everyone is trained and competent there are different schools of course check out degrees fees can become an issue of your choice and some may be in service or abroad as usual nothing's simple it's all a part of the grand unraveling that must take place before the new line can be introduced : prepare now not be shocked when the music starts the year's fashions may feature pins and nails.

# DELETE 13

Rest the plot, shadow, cut to your chase — you mean the you, the I, thou, we, us. Yes : not to play the Zeno game but you might as well know there will always be a space between us, you spend so much time looking for ladders or leaping into the air with blind faith which is exactly that. stone blind. ladders or leaps, they are the same old trick, a move outside the farthest province of speech, can't you find something more colloquial we're not talking warm fuzzies here but plain-edged lingo with a handle on each word which each can hold, to hold to as the only way across the space of words cut loose from words, it's your umbilical with your only kind, listen as carefully as you ever have, noise is what you'll hear not heavenly choirs : oh it can be sweet music for the deprived, the oppressed, but after that funny feeling you're right back where you started from, out of the loop by social design, not even Bill's old boy "the undertaker's understrapper" makes the cut : best tend to your cooking and hope it doesn't burn when a cloud of unknowing spills over you, shake it off as best you can it may be nothing more than a sign of age : Oh : Lord , Laddie/Lady/LaDazzle-o-Mine speak up now or forever hold your piss : stare at a mirror some day and ask yourself if there's really a lesson to be learned or taught : it's a sick trick you teach us Mister Quick so take your peep show passion for the real and carry that infection from port to port : finally : push off, all oars flashing, over a legendary sea *owotthehellmite,* you know the story but you don't know how to spell : that dolphin off the port bow came to talk to you but quickly learned you are no conversationalist being limited to brute fight or flight : yes and no : OK OK don't ride the obvious into the cardboard sky : did you expect to show up on the top forty? well forget it your passport won't accept that stamp.

# DELETE 20

You, an anachronism without knowing it, one who given the case file of your time, was never really a working part of it : you think you worked until your knuckles broke? Historically you know of such phenomena and that they constitute a large, large club, but then you've never won the lottery and only a killjoy would say you've never bought a ticket : it's your own affair how close to a floor named reality you choose to live, from there it's circumstance, contingency, not to be confused with imminence or grace : are charades worth it? of course they are, so are parades, they circulate the blood : but don't get in the wrong line, you'll end up a stranger and lose your irreplaceable place in life, in national security, national interest, how can anyone go wrong? Ask the dumb question, the sucker word, *national,* what does that mean? there is the national interest, there are the national forces to make sure the national interest is secure and there are those in whose name this is done and who pay the bills, you among them, that's how it works : he died today : "I am not a crook" no but we are all criminals : enough said : are you through with this lecture now? : you say you learned this at the pentagon? Don't give me mystic shapes or powers out of this world, come down to earth, buddy, there are graves to be dug, no, not in the national interest but your own : watch your step getting out, the elevator's not quite level with the floor : the building of course is air-tight and even pollen free : do try to look busy all day long : walk with a piece of paper in your hand : what if de Tocqueville's "mob" found the "interest" wasn't theirs? Oh, there'd be hell to pay and you might have to use the stairs to get away : but you have forgotten the tanks : the "mob" wouldn't stand a chance : your "leaders" are in another country by now : the helicopter on the roof, the corporate jet : the national interest went with them as they flew : go bury the dead when the cinemax cameras roll : a piece of work : you can't remember how you were assigned to tend the cell where conscience lives, rent free.

# D E L E T E 30

Time to turn over the hour glass old hat : the eternal return : the up-side down again : come on down the descent is steady sandy desolate blood into rivers dim ancestral claims of race and sect a famine-driven mass will fling bat-like against the knights of power ghost faces with overwhelming arms at hand : Caesars there will be to hold the stage until downfalling sand smothers their swords : it's a metaphor that leaves the question open of how the hour glass gets flipped about: "a rearranger of the furniture" : an assumption cynical and human : a blindfold for the passage of an age — hence — dump it in the metaphysics bin and be done not with this morning but with your discount shelf "philosophies of life" that shop has been foreclosed and millions robbed they dropped just once that happy painted face : depressions and euphoria are waves that only the most expert immortals ride gods because they never come to shore sand streams throughout their dreams and brings then back buried alive in being — faith's equinox — where to begin? try motion mother of souls and galaxies her arch-browed visage wreathed in skulls and keening for the dead : Kali and Mary and the Wheel of Fortune Queen running the letters which make up the world and therein are the names of all things hidden this is the day by day you've spoken for with luck you'll make it to the bonus round : where are you going? we have a door to nowhere : the flood of language passes from your grasp babelized and rain-tongued with your sacrificial blood into the earth : caught between window and the screen the noise is deafening : the words are hid : a catastrophe of dialects : a crossfire of opinion borne by light : take it slow and easy one breath at a time realize there is no recovery from this step forward : don't let a time-out fool you : you were never in the game no matter what numbers were announced : call for a replay : the outcome will always be "too close to call."

# DELETE 43

They're there all right : what you call scars : they're living proof that somehow buttons do get pushed : but don't expect a wizard behind each drape — that was your golden age of compromise – how long has this charade been going on? And where is Kansas on your psychic map? Just because you cruise the information super-highway you drowse and dream you're going somewhere : the freeway exits are few and far between the trick is not to get black flagged but keep on running until the black and white appears it's over then and there is no appeal : some day your deed may be as glowing legends of action heroes war and domination to the max a slow turn of the wheel will groan before your type (not kind) will strain through corporate global action up the hill with firepower enough to win the game : as before flood waters rise and drown the crops deserts take over farms suburbs cities wind driven sand invade the sacred places vaults of the dead secret vaults of money that armageddon claptrap once again it is such a tired complaint. An old Lament : all passion may be spent but hatred grows unsatisfied until the final bone : then waltz me around again Willie the band's gone home they were out of tune and merely moneycentric : may god be with you and me as well? A pillar between us a boundary not to be crossed not particles unbroken waves of time but rosaries around\ the spinning wheels of prayer : a match burst alive is snuffed in a high wind : hope for that instant a lifetime's loss : light vanishes but not for lack of wanting : wind is a given of the open field as real as that kicked rock and Dr. Johnson's sorely battered foolish gouty toe : this is not the shop for opiates or answers : mark well the local household gods the vacuum cleaner or the microwave : outside there are familiars to be met bug-eyed Jim Lizzard . Coyote . Raven . Fox their familiarity is not with you : open your exile's pretentious house they will not enter and settle by the fire — that's how the story goes into a future more absurd than a wakened version of the past : highwire your way, trickster, across that canyon : follow the aleatory, manual in hand.

A void — a natural wonder of the world much talked about but never photographed — standing in place like so much we live and die by — reflexive as the customs of your birth — remember there is a sunny side to the street why not cross over put on a happy face? A winter solstice hoards its fill of light but then it's over you can go on again to a close up for TV — welcome to sirens and blood — mud — as always — when the winter comes turn up the thermostat and lock the doors it's not as if you've made a moral choice — today is simply not *your* tragedy — this *I* we speak of is fish-slippery and seldom caught and out of its own water it will die — its startles will slow and stop laboratory tested : you're not yourself a volunteer and cannot mourn a world you never knew old pinball slaphappy is your daily game you may reach home a winner maybe not you'll know when your jackpot lights flash and go out : it is a journey through the beaches rocks and fields of thought daily experiments life upon life : that which must be : dreadful joyous : ecstasy and despair fumble with abstractions paper thin useless arrows in a labyrinth dead ends blind alleys the obvious overlooked : progress has no measure in this game so let the dice which a dead god cannot roll spill out directions for your useful day data is the spark and stuff of daily work : polity is useless in this game : there are wars primitive wars technical ghettoes like plasma held in a ring of arms : slowly lift your eyelids to the dark : it is morning but in winter's heavy light : all night you have stretched out upon the trash of centuries death squads prepare you for your scholar's day " you have as they say your work cut out for you but whoa! that's life : is it time for lunch so soon? take stock of what you think you know be quiet and observe the scene what you see is what you get : nothing less or more.

# DELETE 45

There must be something left standing at twilight something to point to : color : mother of pearl : black plastic streets from a bone cold all day rain : the morning's electric blinding daylight confrontation gives way to ambush and death by memory : is there nothing left to hold us together? : uneasy truce between mind and gut : and just before the twilight vanishes belief steps forward unsupported strong and strides on trackless paths into the dark : do you believe this stuff? does it take you back? : a millennium lures the doomsday sayers front and center : the only available novelty : behold! : the monotony of cruelty : you're used to that each medication time : watch Nietzsche the first to reach the finish line he keeps on running thinking he will fly : better to keep moving dizzy : a household dervish : otherwise you will collapse into yourself become invisible too dense to live : each game with death is zero sum minus the safety net of strategy : should we form a ring of dancers 'round a fire? Dance is the perfect signature of being a costume change it will come 'round again with signal fires that pass from hill to hill : boil you pot on that mystery my heart : between light and dark abused convenient poles where explanations always simmer in tides of daily pleasure and of pain : there is a self confinement order in the house of custom : be catatonic there in a made-to-order jacket that must be stretched to join a ring of dancers and your peers : can you accept your bankruptcy of state? Come off that pundit's podium : be nice : that's all that ever really will be asked of you : meanwhile the password and the stockades appear : underground of course : you will end up in one appropriate to your pedigree and class : it is brutally simple a millennial scenario that can be set aside by sudden missile alliances you never dreamed about from coalitions your strategies forgot : but why this futuristic shit into the fan? come home to papa home to papa do! : it's easy to mimic the prodigal son even when there's no home left and patriarchs are not for hire : has it occurred to you that truth may be your last deceptive move?

Hypothesis : history's unmade bed : Spengler's age of caesars may return as ice cream tradition melts under the sun : the power is off again . campfires are lit but don't present a silhouette to life : you can be mistaken in your blackened bulk your guilt and good works your wishing well are bullet-proof as ghosts you cannot touch nor taste : you've reached your last goodbye : hope against hope : this thing is nothing new my daily dust : it's just that now it's happening to you : with Whitman as pied piper you are the rat that followed in his rough American wake : oh "ring dem bells" for bloody battle time : and pitch with King Billy your hoard of bomb balls in : you were right about the center Mister Yeats, a new *centre* is on the stage today a free agent all-pro and promised to the highest bidder : and civilized as god : somewhere truth's shadow turns away and just in time : move to the sunny side you'll say again, : but that my captain is where the sun don't shine : face it the air's gone out of your Pratt and Whitney's : there's no point in falling downstairs once more : you cannot prove it was an accident : a bureaucratic light cannot penetrate this far into the tar pits : dear traveler the price is right for you although you have no choice : look where your questions have brought you . life support systems unplugged . the night nurse no longer calls your name : in the shadows fumes of melancholia gather and rehearse : before all caring ends.

3

# CHECK POINT

"Lord, when shall we be done changing?"
Herman Melville — letter to
Nathaniel Hawthorne, November 17, 1851


Assembled in faded garments of our words
a century's splintered aftermath
tabbed for retrieval pressed
between the mind's eye and the heart's desire
a collision of forgetfulness
and a desperate "need to know"
without compassion meaning
collapses like a wall whose building
has been bombed rubble falls in upon itself
lodged in the debris of particulars
disposable truths : political reality : nothing
flows easily : not water : not fire
not even our sacred envelope of air.

We have brought our bloodland ways
into a century we shall not outlive
opened sores upon this body of earth

Aomori · Augsburg · Baedeker Blitz · Bahrain · Barrow-in-Furness
Belfast · Belgrade · Berlin · Birmingham · Braunschweig · Bremen
Breslau · Brighton · Bristol · Bucharest · Budapest · Caen · Calcutta
Cardiff · Chemnitz · Chişinău · Chongqing · Clydebank · Cologne
Coventry · Danzig · Darmstadt · Darwin · Dresden · Dublin · Duisburg
Düsseldorf · Essen · Foggia · Frampol · Frankfurt · Frascati · Fukui
Fukuoka · Fukuyama · Gelsenkirchen · Gibraltar · Gifu · Greenock
Guangzhou · Haifa · Hamamatsu · Hamburg · Hanau · Heilbronn
Helsinki · Hildesheim · Hiratsuka · Hiroshima · Hull · Innsbruck
Kaiserslautern · Kassel · Kobe · Königsberg · Kure · Leipzig · Liverpool
London · Lübeck · Mainz · Malta · Manchester · Manila · Mannheim
Minsk · Mito · Munich · Nagaoka · Nagasaki · Nagoya · Naha · Nanjing
Naples · Narva · Nottingham · Numazu · Nuremberg · Omuta · Osaka
Pearl Harbor · Pforzheim · Ploiesti · Plymouth · Podgorica · Prague

Rabaul · Remscheid · Rome · Rothenburg ob der Tauber · Rotterdam
Saarbrücken · Salzburg · Schaffhausen · Schwäbisch Hall · Schweinfurt
Sendai · Shanghai · Sheffield · Shizuoka · Singapore · Sofia · Southampton
Stalingrad · Stettin · Stuttgart · Swansea · Taipei · Tallinn · Tel Aviv
Thessaloníki · Tokyo · Toyama · Toyohashi · Treviso · Tsu · Ujiyamada
Ulm · Vienna · Warsaw · Wesel · Wieluń · Wuppertal · Würzburg · Yawata
Yokohama · Zadar · Zagreb

Area bombardment · Aerial bombing of cities · Terror bombing ·
V-weapons


Into a void always on download
faith into faith all structures of belief
trembling not one wall left unshaken.

Say, "Tea kettle or dying animal"
rhetoric against the house arrest
of age nettle sting of memory
that in an old man loses out to sleep.

What is the past but a failed retrieval
of what at the time seemed relevant and true
arriving through a tangle of dendrites
an invasion of beta-amyloid as reported
in The New York Times and hardening to dogma
— mumble mumble mumble      pop —
at last you have explained it all.


"If I want the door to turn
the hinges must stay put."
not that a life depends upon it
but that it works that way the door
remains closed and the hinges quiet.
A wolf within escapes his chain
and shows his teeth and claims his turf.

"Set keel to breakers," that optimistic metaphor

and with it the voyage itself until a full circle of the horizon
reveals nothing as in fog this blindness is my inheritance
marginal at best mostly memory and flat-out inability
a distorting lens as with a winter's storm that hurls water
against the west-facing windows obliterating hillside
ocean and a bent wild gesturing tree
at one time I would have walked the cliff pretending
to be closer to the event but not now I'd stumble
into another metaphor : Old Man Lost in a Storm.

Gimbal broken and the compass lost
a different equilibrium arrives off-center
and never for a frozen moment real
but grown tipsy with reality an overdose of self
with fluid navigation points, false poles
of a non-navigable world.

It is a misdirected enterprise to call upon the dead for wisdom
we have their words but the speakers are just that: dead
along with their enfeebled gods and ghostly shrines
yet the sword slices the same meat of the same animal
that fought at Troy and the ghost that rushes from us is the same.

We have our seasons and our instruments of perishable joy
our shadow metaphysic of the transient soul
our virtual realities dislodge the arbitrary gods.
We build our temples with the stones at hand.

# GRIEF OCTAVES

(*Ruth McNerney Moore, 1922 – 1997*)

1. Waterfall: Russian Gulch State Park

Recently I've been receiving lessons in death,
how a shallow stream swallows light and spits it out
in jagged splinters. image-broken mirrors.
This is one of the ways life works, indirect
choices that lead unerringly to determined ends.
The trail is slipperiest near the waterfall,
but every step leads this way only. Take care,
once you're here, there's no place else to be.


2. Sunset

Yes, it is spectacular. I look on it as a phenomenon of nature, which it
is.
We would argue, "Is the sunset greater because we watch it together?"
You always held to the affirmative. Tonight's sunset may be equal
to any we had ever watched, there can be no argument.
Something is terminally wrong.
There are cataracts of color that fall within me.
A paradox: how can an exterior sunset appear,
in an instant, so *interior?*


3. Poetry

Hourly I need it more and more, this stop-
troubled-time, to find stars behind cloud cover
or the hidden colors of a fallen leaf, or
navigation beacons moved by stealth
to places I have never been before.
I need the shell game words, the pea, to make
a second's worth of narrative, a landmark
renamed, a present tense that stretches shadows far.

4. Knick-knacks

There are household gods we shared.
It took our joint imagination squared
to produce them, sill dwellers mostly,
some on shelves. They've gone ghostly.
The once present bulk of them is hollow.
There was one the slightest wind would shake and rattle
and cause the dog to bark at gods misunderstood,
perhaps. He still barks at the vacant window sill wood.


5. Ashes, Ashes

It is a morning for making up to things:
a universe from galaxies of crumbs
from which the bread was cut,
English toffee left on its plain paper,
burrs that the dog brought in.
bark from the wood brought in
to the place where the fire takes place,
to the flammable commonplace.


6. Stumbling in the Market

Plain to see, the can of peaches
does not propose it is found or lost.
I pick up a can of peaches. The check out
clerk agrees with me about the label.
We have spoken before and may again,
not as functionaries but as players
within a function we accept. I shall
attentively take note if there is change.

7. Hour Glass

Nameless, the next grain through the hourglass.
This happens out in the open world, once only.
Never again that event in that final way, a
*Grosse fuge,* that ends and does not begin again.
Walk away from it chilled in silence
empty as all space, vulnerable as the passing light.
Echoes are for information only,
never to be turned over for that event again.


8. Wild Honeysuckle

There is that which, having traveled far, returns
although not native to this place — wild honeysuckle,
sweet vernal grass — and there is that which, although
far traveled, does not return. The name holds
in the language, but we will search for it in vain,
crowded out of life, a glory never again seen, the
legend of it memorialized, filed under incidents past.
Today, make do with hedge-nettle and scarlet pimpernel.

# GOLGOTHA

Memory of an empty cavespace
displacement from a page, the word
sweet inwit of sense that this life
cannot speak to death, ever.

Remember an empty mindspace : after :
abandoned to reconstruction's failure;
miracle has no witness, pale evening primrose,
another overnight event, gone by sunrise.

# BEACHHEAD

Mother of vicissitudes, brood
Above these fretful grasses in the sand,
The wind tangles them, matting blade and stem,
Kleenex and candy wrappers embrace and cling.

Mother of complaints and inward envies, cover
With your bright veil death's imitative pose,
The sleepers, mouth open under the itching sun,
Sunlight scratching on a glass paved sea.

Mother of week-ends and movie magazines,
Rewrite, keep clean, withhold, restore to history
A memory of ourselves, foot-firm and toasty warm
Upon this stretch of sorrows sliding toward the sea.

# Remembering Wallace Stevens

*On CNN at 6:38 PM EST (2:38 AM on Thursday Jan 17 in Iraq)*
*Operation Desert Storm began.*

Perhaps, as Stevens wondered, apples in heaven
Do not fall, an embarrassment of hope:
To anticipate, in joy or dread, leaf spiral
Or shadow on sundials like pistols, deadly
As unseasonable frost, and cocked
To fire upon each sighting of the sun.
Frost has invaded the metropolis of trees,
Alley by alley, the city will be laid waste.

What's left then with this wrestling with words?
Exhaustion marks each morning with a scar.
In blindness is safety: arrows from heaven
Spread death like a blanket for lovers,
Sulfurous hours paint the wind with fog.
Sunrise and sunset notch our time-stick deeper,
Sea grass on the sand dunes burns, the night sky
Spasms in fire, only the mind leaves the body;

And only on condition that the body stay
At home, "charred beyond recognition," ashes
Aloft in the winds or altered to blind fish
In the coldest depths of the sea, why not, why not!
Mind is body as birds are air, both need
A medium to trace their arcs. They find
No handhold in the circling of the stars.
Night falls in fire. Baghdad burns like straw.

# HERE

There is a story of a populous valley
always on the other side, the hills are sand color
under what cannot be called a sheltering sky
enameled into a pale blue glaze, the sea
is distant but can be sensed from here.

Years ago victory was declared
in this new daily invented place, although
daily a battle against a desert must be
engaged, new scripts written, laid out
on the water table, quickly absorbed.

# STANDING BEFORE PICASSO'S "BOY LEADING A HORSE"

The horse does not threaten the nude boy
whose shy teen-aged bravado stares
straight ahead as if to say, "Look
what I've got." The horse, all muscled power
and animal pride, is willing to be led
into the illuminating light, the rose-
pink omnipresent air of the gallery.
Look again, the room is fogged. The paintings
and their accompanying texts have disappeared,
the larger than four by seven frame is gone,
the painting I thought I saw was memory
and not the painting I could not see hanging
on the white wall; until the boy and horse
brushed past me, faintly odorous and warm.

# "Turning God Into One Devil of a Problem"

"The way you use the word 'God' does not show them
*whom* you mean — but rather *what* you mean."
Ludwig Wittgenstein, "On Culture and Value."
Translated by Peter Finch

I.

At first light
fact follows fact
into the visible

point to it
before the words
begin the pretense
that language
is a picture
of the world
and God is all
that is the case.

Inside the language game
there is no room for doubt,

change the rules or stay
indentured to God forever.

2.

Remember the Golden Mountain
that does not exist?
This may be the same story
told and retold as in
*"can* be shown *cannot* be said."

Myth follows myth into belief.
That box is full and unavailable,

the Devil is with the word,
a tired romancer at the limits
of thought, a tag-a-long-
word-creature, a banker
with foreclosure and
the sour breath of time
upon his lips.

The trouble with everything
is that it's true.

"That is God," said Stephen.
"A shout in the street."
Yes, that too.

# WITTGENSTEIN AT A POW WOW

The first step is forward to the blooded earth
and the earth responds, the foot lifts obedient
to the drum (this is a description, not a theory)
in magic there is no time nor is there error
but here are practices and miracles that absorb
all history rising in the wind-twisted dust,
in a social occasion which occupies the whole of time.

Thunder from the four corners of an unfamiliar world,
with high lightning falsetto song, and dancers, dancers
speaking stories of creation and the diabetic present,
not in sequence (there is no progress in magic) but in the grass,
water, breath, and earthly chapel of things as they clearly are.

Within the connections (perspicuous presentation as W has it)
there is nothing provisional, it is a way of seeing the world,
a recognition of connections that are plainly there: foot
to the earth and a lifting up, blood pulse in answer to a drum,
from tribal plenty and solidarity to unemployment and alcohol,
a story of destruction and the glory of the fancy dancer, one story.

Judge as you choose from the safety of a point of view, life
is not an hypothesis to be proved (it is plain as the nose on your face).

In Arlee, Montana time split open and all history swept into the
    bleachers,
magic (not by magic) possessed a visitor who wept and could not stop as
    life after
 life, death after death connected, connected in one vision
of how it is and has always been as in a nearby shelter gamblers' songs
    summoned
 power into breath warmed, hand rubbed, soon to be tossed bones.

4

# A Prefatory Note

Over the past several years I have been acutely aware of my failing vision. I was, however, unprepared to face the emotional devastation brought on by the loss and my receipt in mid summer of 2013 of a letter confirming that I was now "legally blind."

Motivated by a mix of precedent and curiosity I began to write sonnets about becoming blind. Old age became a closely related subject. I use the term sonnet loosely. The only consistent formal element is that each of the poems consists of 14 lines.

What is most interesting to me in this venture is that I attempt to write the poems in ordinary language, not in the sense of ordinary and poetic language, but ordinary in the sense of common speech bordering, at times, on cliché.

# THE OTHER SIDE OF LIGHT

It is not a fair exchange, light for dark,
So much remains on the other side of sight,
A world lost is never a fair exchange.
Memory, like an out-of-date theme park,
Coughs up once familiar tunes gone strange
And foreign in this quickly falling night.
There is no comfort in the loss of sight
Nor hope nor promise in what's left of light.

Plain facts are best expressed in simple speech.
Once disentangled from the world's embrace
The hard edged visible world is out of reach.
A world is lost, but life comes face to face
With life on-going and does not stay
To measure loss but quickly moves away.

# Lately Removed

It is the furniture that's odd — it floats
In heavy syrup-space and adds nothing
(although the world overflows with furniture)
To the history of furniture, nothing except
The counter attack of things lately removed
From sight. There is recognition: a couch,
A table. This is, however, provisional until
Knocked into with the usual result:
A splash of tears, a reach into the past
For objects firmly anchored as, for example
Furniture of the ordinary not the floating kind.
I have lost touch with a familiar world
Become passing strange, increasingly remote
With the absurdity of furniture afloat.

# ONE DEMAND

Of course the feeling is not accurate
(as if that made a difference!), but yes,
It does, and although illegitimate
The feeling is as strong as all else
In a world of fancy and of fact.
Paper on thin paper, it takes a while
For copy paper to become a stack,
Followed by extraordinary clutter
Which, in turn, is followed by a pile.
And all at once a chorus starts to mutter,
A history-changing moment is at hand.
Be sure to keep it simple, make one demand.
It's immolation time, one for the ages.
The headline: Writer Smothers In Own Pages.

# GET USED TO IT

"Get used to it." No, I won't.
This was all I could think of while
Passing through a well remembered door
(it opens *in* not *out*, there is no sill)
A detail now wrapped in layers of gauze
Plus endless other unrealities.
This has become the order of the day
And every day now on against my will.

To have it otherwise would now be called
An optical illusion. You can pass through
A solid wall, it takes a single door.
A negotiation with reality
Is to ride the in-breath into death. Blind
I long for that other-sighted world still.

# Hasten Sundown

Draw back the curtains and reveal the day.
A sudden inflood of the sun repels
At first, but softens lacking all detail.
I undertake a morning ritual
of reconciliation with a world
gone forever, absent without leave.
"O lost and by the wind grieved,"
These words stay with me as my vision fails.

I could close the curtains and restore the dark
But that would only hasten sundown
The abandonment of light. Face up to it:
There are no choices to be made in this
Wide existential world of gray
Encounters day after fading day.

# WHAT?

What had I expected of old age?
A graceful exit, all obligations met?
A dignified withdrawal from the scene?
Plain truth, I didn't think about it.

Anticipation seldom matches fact.
I expect a world to be as a world has been,
Never this gross abandonment of means
To live life – signs, sounds and the touch of things.

I recall a dark wood and a labyrinth.
Distinguished travelers have felt the cold
Chill of things to come and have moved on
To unplanned destinations, illusive goals.

Legally blind, I hoard what small light stays
Against failing hope, illuminated days.

# NAMING

Of disappearing worlds and sundry matters
I have become a traitorous informant,
Even to myself, doubtful about what's there
And what's been cast adrift and forgotten.
Mount Tamalpais and the tidal marsh
Are presences that cannot guide my steps
Toward mountain meditation or salt-marsh
Naming of the rarer water birds.

The last entry — Black Crowned Night Heron —
Was months and months and months ago. I
Remember the round-shouldered look of the bird
I cannot see today.
While from the mountain top a sense of height
And space fails to refresh my eyes with sight.

# INTO THE LIGHT

They have dimension and detail, but lack
Substance; nor do they speak a human tongue.
Full seven feet, these bedside sentinels
Stand their ground a moment at first light
Before vanishing into a tapestry
Hung on the west bedroom wall.
Apparitions or angels? Equally unreal.
Equally an optical fact of sight.

It's best to be matter of fact about
This kind of thing. My library of a brain
Supplies the images. They resemble
Descriptions from a Jungian seminar
But this disclaimer doesn't get me far,
Daily, at first light, there they are.

# TRINKETS

I cannot make it to the end of night.
A heavy dark envelopes the last light,
Dulls the trinkets of a blinding day,
Drops them, does not pause, but moves away
Into an unknown and galactic place.
I have no world of reference or grace
To base a life upon, reduced to seeing
Grizzly bears aloft and angels dancing.

Invention has its limits and cannot
Restore what memory, blindsided, has forgot.
As line by line a universe of print
Vanishes silently without complaint.
Against the sweet persistencies of breath,
It is the sum of losses equals death.

# ACCESS DENIED

Print accompanies the best of days,
On call at any hour, day or night.
There is no equal to what a page displays
Of fact and fancy, scattered left and right,
Not as a picture of what's present there
But as a means of making sense of it,
A way of seeing the commonplace and rare
With memory as a find of retrofit.

Now access to that world has been denied
Except for memory which must be fed
By the very world that has become a hide
And seek affair. It goes straight to my head
Which overflows with thick nostalgic stuff
As I take up the game of Blind Man's Bluff.

# A DARK HOUSE

My limited engagement with a self
Has had a longer than expected run,
A closing date, a dark house lie ahead,
But these familiar rituals of life
Are prematurely dark. It is stumble time
Although the scenery remains the same.
Personas keep their costumes, lose their voice.
Bewildered, they whisper in the wings
Whereas the self remains alone on stage,
At once the actor and the dramaturge.
Then who is this I half-see in a mirror,
The center blacked-out, light at the edge?
Entire worlds vanish with the lost of sight
Prospero's island, Lemuria, sweet daylight.

# THE FAMILIAR HAS TAKEN LEAVE

Responding to a world turned outside in
Requires a fresh agility of will
And a surreal mode of thought, both distant
When the world was visible and real.
The only carry-over is the sound:
The hollow clatter of the commonplace,
Ancestral voices, sepulchral complaints
From many sources now invisible.

This is the most dispassionate I can be.
The familiar has taken leave with all I know
And what is left is mostly echo fading,
Never to return. What takes shape then
Is virtual and is a world apart
Assembled half by memory, half by art.

5

# EXILE

Herein an addiction of evidence
even to "I know that is a chair"

a word-severed disorderly withdrawal

remember baggage   remember
to take it with you   all you can bear.

# SCAFFOLDS

## I. SAFETY NET

*"Here it is, already saucered and blowed."*
*...a child's introduction to coffee (c. 1924)*

From near forgotten voices
almost another language
another form of life ...

*"Shame! There's enough left on your plate
to feed Coxes' Army."*

...too soon hard times
another form of life
stunned into animal silence ...

*"We shot Uncle Wiggly."*
        A week of hysteria followed.
Unreliable child.

*"Been a snake, t'would have bit you."*


Obvious from the empty shelves
the marathon dancers falling
into stories of suicides
into dreams of falling
into A Theater of America
new sets already fading
torn in strategic places.

*"He said, 'I hate war and so does Eleanor,
but we won't be safe till everybody's dead.'"*

Socialists have no taste.
        Capitalists have no soul.
A production for our time.
        Opening soon.

## II. PLATFORM BURIAL

*(for men of a certain age, the Question:*
*what branch of the service were you in?)*

Spring winds sweep clean
    a century's burial fields
burst open in keening
    wrestled to a prairie wind
snagged in the Breaks
    unheard in the compounds
the fortresses of state.

Old ways and old men
    deathly combination
ending in rats and corpses
    unspeakable half-
century from Horse Marines
    to Little Boy
destroyer of worlds.

*＊＊＊*

Four notched poles firmly
    planted on a high bluff
in bleak unforgiving light
    placed to receive
a century's warriors
    — all of them —
in dress uniforms and ribbons
    tight-wrapped in their nation's
flag an ignorant blasphemy
    buffalo robes stained
into nationhood
    Indian removal
unnatural war.

*＊＊＊*

73

Never such an airy burial
  such a clean display
at their leisure the ravens
  eat their fill
a story too well known
  to be understood.

✳✳✳

"The ultimate terror
  of a world on fire,"
a common statement
  that misses the cause
of ultimate terror
  and its trigger
neither fission or fusion
  but a human fingertip.

(it was the custom among some mourners
to cut off a finger joint to show their grief)


III. A-TUG-OF-WAR

An address and driving directions, that's all he had and all he could remember about where he was headed. A fool's errand?

His first response was nausea. Small wonder, considering the unpleasant taste of the dry cactus buds. A stained sheet of three quarter inch plywood was an improvised table that held several large bottles of soft drinks, a quart of vodka (half gone), and two bottles of bulk white wine. Resembling hors d'oeuvres of dates or olives, a bowl of peyote buttons completed the offering. The early nausea overcome, he stretched out full length on one of the oversized couches in the room intending to relax and enjoy an "experience."

The first sensation was of internal pressure seeking to exit via his navel. "Weird!" Automatically he put his hand over his belly button. It made no difference. The sensation continued but his attention was drawn to a screen on which two white lines were beginning to assume the outline of a human. Only then did he realize that the screen and his own body were, somehow, synchronized. It seemed a matter of indifference that he was now in a screening room. What did hold his attention was his growing anxiety over where he was.

He seemed no longer an inhabitant of his own body. Instead, he was in a screening room — a spectator for what was going on within his body. Against a vibrating dark purple background two lines emerged. The lines could have been neon tubing except that they were pliable and alive. Slowly and against resistance the lines began to trace in cartoon fashion the outline of a body above the sketch of a body he recognized as his own. "It's an animated film." He heard his own voice booming out this message.

His attention became fixed on the outline of the second body. On the screen it appeared to draw its energy from the original. His body. "Nonsense, of course, but a clever conceit for the film." Again, he heard his own voice booming out, this time with the echo chamber in full play: "nonsense…nonsense…nonsense." His confusion was momentary. He awoke only to be overcome by the realization that a desperate battle had begun. A third body was pushing its way into existence and as it fought to emerge as a twin of the second body from which it drew its "strength," the original body seemed to become a mere sketch, a drawing, a representation not a reality. "Whoa!" he heard himself say, "This is not an entertainment." It became clear that he was being sucked dry of life. A momentary panic followed, but in the same moment a purely instinctual will to live took hold. The cartoon lines expanded only to be "willed" to contract and return to his body. "It's a metaphysical test of will!" He may have tried to sound clever, but there was more than a touch of panic in his voice.

All he remembered of the struggle is that it required maximum effort. It was not a test of muscular strength, although that too was involved in the contractions needed to hold on to and eventually return the outline of the body to its primal source. The sense of achievement and relief at having returned the body to the body, the self to its bodily home exceeded all other thoughts and associations as he descended the back stairway leading to the parking lot and his car.

## IV. JACKSTRAW

There it stands. A hunk of it. In dense print.
*Inheritance:* "Vietnam's burnt villages"
a lump of coal for the planet
a bloody story already forgotten
In this century of perpetual war.

What was "lived through" and what not?
the answers change with the year
and with the time of day racing
toward a still point never reached
except in print. A quiet book unread.

The familiar is the first to leave the field
the road twisting away and out of sight
shedding the visible remains of time
perishable as history and of equal rot
afterscent of what at the time made sense.

Take to the hills at sunrise on the eastern rim
a corona of orange light as the sun slowly
shoulders upward — met by a jackrabbit –
broad ears aflame with daybreak
a visitation from a nourishing world.

*Annihilation* — prime indeterminate –
shattering sunlight from ordinary earth
we are of the species that foretells its own
destruction an ultimate imperial
  vanity never to be read or spoken.
Until from myriad absences of love
there is another story to be told
of languages assembled in fragile peace
dissembled at first touch approached
once more all hope and promise left behind.

From jumbled numbers of absurd events
propose a grand pavane of balance a dance

of options contradictions structural texts
withdraw the jackstraw of transforming love
take care to shoulder the first morning light.

# LANDSCAPE WITH FIGURES

The full anxiety of immanence
bodied in the weight of ever arriving

empirical given wholly to be understood
within an ontology of the very small

what can be said of the world     fact-bundle
spoken     less than gestures naming.

# DREAMS

I had hoped for clarity
a narrowing down
to an ever smaller field.

Unprepared

I can no longer
identify myself
in any remembered place.

# A FAMILY AFFAIR

*In a manner of speaking*

A life is what is said of it
not star light but the story of
sun centered stars or so we say
again and again and believe it
keep your distance or be burned
into a scabbed disfigurement
of what so we are told makes sense
the authenticating angels have been
paid off cannot blow a whistle
are silent as stone angels must be.

In ceremony at the solstice
lay out the ornaments of the years
and say. "This is a world."

*Of words*

Winter came suddenly with no surprise
one daybreak the maps stiffened
ache became visible we were prepared
through evening lectures and the internet,
we were not prepared to live it, yet.

*Velcro mind stay with me on this trip*

Stay with me now as the cosmologist
dazzles with starlight just arrived
from before the earth had settled into orbit
double occupancy for the one space
a great migration of the yes and no of case.

*Velcro mind stay with me*

Move grandly into the gathering of words
and measurements — a reach — hand span —

light speed — pressures that lift mountains break seas
from the grand uproar of the first event
in a non-detectable nil of time.

*Velcro mind*

Hold to your post-mathematics album
that measures a world in years of light
in geologic pages of stone
hang on to it and it to you.

*Velcro*

Lost memory of a sudden taking leave
a kite caught in winter branches
(have we not been here before?)
remember a *commodius vicus of recirculation*
and rejoyce.

# INDEX

Among the irretrievable wastes of thought
breath beneath notice          assumed present

systemic exhaustion of the possible
heart's pestilence of life inmost pulse

bear the unbearable     wear the world's way
the executioner's hood  a prisoner of it.

# WHERE

to be     to come to

find the windblown sand
I become in my dream

upon waking.

# APART FROM IT

"No, it is impossible to convey the life-sensation
of any given epoch of one's existence."
                    Joseph Conrad, *The Heart of Darkness*


The angel of memory is forgetful,
does not keep score, but plays the game
as if all existence is at stake,
as if every waking is the first
to break the freeze-frame
moments, all frozen smiles
and tintype mimicry, fading
come daylight, so quickly gone.

＊＊＊

Keeper of fiction as the pure event,
an angelic imperfection of a perfect game,
the aeroplane in the box of Cracker Jack.

Never the closer for the saying of it,
locked into freedom, a universe of one
arrested, imprisoned in time past.

＊＊＊

Hillcrest, stucco, French doors and garage, fireless cooker; an entry into
the new century, certain to be the most glorious. The Yanks will make the
difference. Wheat will win the War. Patriotism has a patent on prosperity,
just wait and see. The Yanks will encamp in Washington, the Bonus
Army, but that's getting ahead of the story, times were good before the
fall. From the sleeping porch in the new house, new everything, a child
heard a scream. "Go to sleep. It was only a rabbit, probably an owl got
it." Ever after, he was poised for flight. "Too delicate for his own good."
Such was the verdict of the doctor, the neighborhood, his school; his
parents were perplexed — "Nothing seems to be going right, the job, the
house, the child" — a premonition easily fulfilled in 1929. The loudest

voice, the auctioneer's. Home became a matter of month to month rent, a pursuit of anything that paid. The family disappeared under that weight. On the road in broke America. The rumor of jobs was mileage on the road. South to Hamilton. North to St. Joe. East to Connecticut. South to Ohio again. Southeast to Asheville. Far west to Albuquerque, all the way to LA. Tuberculosis took over a mother's life. Travel toward a never defined western dream became a daily hope, along with prayer and healing rituals, alien foods and sputum cups. Life held for another seven on-the-run years ending in LA and a mother's final hemorrhage. Not prayer nor any belief in country or in god survived that fugitive year.

※※※

Face it. There is no getting away from it.
The back roads are packed with waiting sensors.
A spider in my cap panicked and ran.

A church doorway suggested a way out.
Inside, the eye of God reflected candles.
And a mother dead from TB.

An event "not lived through" and therefore
Not found in life. Don't tell me that again!
A slippery metaphysic — the eye of God —

In the narrow daylight of a needle's eye
Reflected intimations never met.
Unreal and sexual at the core of it.

A spider in my hair panicked and ran
But it was only memory
And nightmares past.

※※※

There were other lives to be imitated, perhaps to be lived. Ancestry vanished like a glacier into the sea. There was nothing that was not new or stolen. There were shoes to be tested, paths to be walked. Fainting from hunger, possessed of a larger hunger for the years to come.

\*\*\*

Who pauses to remember?

A further estrangement
in the midst of chance.

\*\*\*

Evening swallows in saw-tooth flying
warn us of night's advance by crying.

They leave although they crowd the sky
no cut or imprint where they fly.

Upon the air each flick of wing
is an accomplished fragile thing,

But grace and art too soon give way
to the exhaustion of the day.

Light gone, the swallows end their flight,
  abandoned, we must face the night.

\*\*\*

North by northeast into the permafrost, the climate change of age. We
are as rhizomes tangled and holding fast, then let go, never let go, moved
beyond to other latitudes and temperatures of place until, deep into the
fiction of a "taking place," a darker fiction of identity takes hold, ever
directed toward the end of it.

\*\*\*

Old Man, breathe-in your daily ration of
sweet air before the wobbly column tumbles:
nine decades, stacked and placed off center,
your building blocks, before the metaphor
collapses to chit-chat evidence of life;
your legs will not support this pilgrimage

admit that this is now and recognize
that this is real as it will ever get.

And then what? The sum of "that which is the case"
becomes a salvaged fiction of the real,
a distillations of belief, held
hard in the indifferent embrace
of chance and circumstance, harder still
in life's divine, obliterating love.

# ACKNOWLEDGMENTS

It has been my good fortune to have extraordinary and generous friends. This is not common in the literary world.

Brenda Hillman and Paul Ebenkamp were the prime movers behind *Writing the Silences* and have continued to work with me on *Particulars of Place*.

Garrett Caples has steered *Particulars of Place* through the many requirements of publication. He is solely responsible for publication of many poems in this collection in magazines ranging from the *Brooklyn Rail* to *Volt*.

Through Garrett Caples I met Cedar Sigo, who has contributed the introduction to *Particulars of Place*. I am especially grateful for his insights into the many facets of my work in both film and poetry.

Stephen Kessler is another friend. Editor of the *Redwood Coast Review*, he has published many poems of mine including four of the *Blindness Sonnets*.

My conversations with each and every one of the persons mentioned are always rewarding and helpful and I am extremely grateful for that.

The most recent friends are Rusty Morrison and Ken Keegan of Omnidawn with whom I have enjoyed working in the preparation of this book.

Some of these poems have appeared in the following publications: *Brooklyn Rail, New American Writing, The Redwood Coast Review, Amerarcana, Volt*.

# NOTES

from "d e l e t e ." This is a selection from fifty prose poems written in the 1980s and early 1990s. "d e l e t e" 1 through 6 were included in *Writing the Silences.*

"Turning God into One Devil of a Problem" is the title of an essay by the Welsh philosopher D. Z. Philips, included in *Covering Religious Concepts: Closing Epistemic Divides,* published by Palgrave Macmillan in 2000.

from *Outcry. Outcry* is a privately printed chapbook consisting of thirty sonnets on blindness.

# ABOUT THE AUTHOR

"Poetry has been and continues to be my lifelong vocation," Richard O. Moore writes. "Fortunately, a secondary interest —filmmaking and public media—has enabled me to pay the inevitable bills." One of the original circle of anarchist poets centered around Kenneth Rexroth in the 1940s—including Robert Duncan, Jack Spicer, Philip Lamantia, Madelaine Gleason, William Everson, James Broughton, and Thomas Parkinson —Moore stopped publishing early on to devote himself to a career in broadcasting, as a co-founder of the first U.S. listener-sponsored radio station, KPFA, and later as an early member of the 6th U.S. public TV station, KQED. Along the way he became an important cinéma vérité filmmaker, directing such works as *Take This Hammer* (1963) featuring James Baldwin; *Louisiana Diary* (1963), documenting the CORE voter registration drive; and the 10-part series *USA: Poetry* (1966), which includes the only sound footage of Frank O'Hara. His later series, *The Writer in America* (1975), chronicled such figures as Toni Morrison, Eudora Welty, and Muriel Rukeyser. The two films he made with Duke Ellington, *Love You Madly* (1967), and *A Concert of Sacred Music* (1967), are the subject of an essay he has contributed to a massive photo-biography of the musician by Steven Brower and Mercedes Ellington, forthcoming from Rizzoli. Moore's first book, *Writing the Silences,* was edited by Brenda Hillman and Paul Ebenkamp and published in 2010 by the University of California. At age 95, he continues to write and lives in Mill Valley, California.

Particulars of Place
by Richard O. Moore

Book cover art and design by Janet Tumpich

Cover typeface: Adobe Jenson Pro.
Interior Typefaces: Trajan Pro and Adobe Garamond Pro

Offset printed in the United States
by Edwards Brothers Malloy, Ann Arbor, Michigan
On 55# Enviro Natural 100% Recycled 100% PCW
Acid Free Archival Quality FSC Certified Paper
with Rainbow FSC Certified Colored End Papers

Omnidawn Publishing
Richmond, California
2014
Rusty Morrison & Ken Keegan, Senior Editors & Publishers
Gillian Olivia Blythe Hamel, Managing Poetry Editor, Book Designer,
& OmniVerse Managing Editor
Cassandra Smith, Poetry Editor & Book Designer
Peter Burghardt, Poetry Editor & Book Designer
Turner Canty, Poetry Editor
Liza Flum, Poetry Editor & Social Media
Sharon Osmond, Poetry Editor & Bookstore Outreach
Juliana Paslay, Fiction Editor & Bookstore Outreach Manager
Gail Aronson, Fiction Editor
RJ Ingram, Poetry Editor & Social Media
Melissa Burke, Poetry Editor & Feature Writer
Sharon Zetter, Poetry Editor & Poetry Editor
Josie Gallup, Feature Writer